Afraid of the Water

MORAY EEL
Dangerous Teeth

by Meish Goldish

Consultant: Rita Mehta, Ph.D.
Postdoctoral Researcher
Section of Evolution & Ecology
University of California
Davis, California

BEARPORT
PUBLISHING

New York, New York

Credits

Cover and Title Page, © David Hall/age fotostock/SuperStock and Rich Carey/Shutterstock; 4, © Andrew Chant; 5, © Jez Tryner/ Image Quest Marine; 6, © Novastock/Photolibrary; 7, © Diane Armstrong/Photolibrary; 8L, © Kit Kittle/Corbis; 8R, © Franco Banfi/ SeaPics.com; 9, © Herb Segars/Animals Animals Enterprises; 10, Courtesy of Rita Mehta; 11, Courtesy of Rita Mehta; 12, © Doug Perrine/SeaPics.com; 13, © Tamsin Eyles/www.tamsineyles.co.uk; 14, © Alf Jacob Nilsen/Bioquatic; 15, © Doug Perrine/SeaPics. com; 17, © Pacific Stock/SuperStock; 18, © Noriaki Yamamoto/Nature Production; 19, © Paul Osmond/www.deepseaimages.com; 20, Photo by Dr. Colin Riordan. Excerpted from Wilderness & Environmental Medicine, Volume 15, No. 3. Used with permission from the Wilderness Medical Society, Salt Lake City, Utah; 21, © age fotostock/SuperStock; 22T, © Redmond Durrell/Alamy; 22B, © J.W. Alker/ imagebroker/Alamy; 24, © Russell swain/Shutterstock.

Publisher: Kenn Goin
Senior Editor: Lisa Wiseman
Creative Director: Spencer Brinker
Photo Researcher: Picture Perfect Professionals, LLC
Design: Dawn Beard Creative

Library of Congress Cataloging-in-Publication Data

Goldish, Meish.
  Moray eel : dangerous teeth / by Meish Goldish ; consultant, Rita Mehta.
      p. cm. — (Afraid of the water)
  Includes bibliographical references and index.
  ISBN-13: 978-1-59716-941-7 (lib. bdg.)
  ISBN-10: 1-59716-941-2 (lib. bdg.)
  1. Moray eel—Juvenile literature. I. Title.

  QL638.M875G65 2010
  597'.43—dc22
                                        2009006725

For more information, write to Bearport Publishing Company, Inc., 101 Fifth Avenue, Suite 6R, New York, New York 10003.
Printed in the United States of America in North Mankato, Minnesota.

122009
120109CG

10 9 8 7 6 5 4 3 2

Contents

A Bad Bite

In 2005, **scuba diving** instructor Matt Butcher and a friend were in the waters off the Similan Islands in Thailand, a country in Southeast Asia. They were looking for Emma, a seven-foot-long (2.1-m) moray eel that instructors often fed when they took tourists diving in the area. Matt had brought a plastic bag filled with mini sausages to give the large fish.

Suddenly, the giant moray swam up behind Matt. She quickly went for the bag of meat. Using her mouth full of razor-sharp teeth, she bit down hard. Instead of biting into the meat, however, she cut right through Matt's hand. He tried to open the fish's mouth to get his hand out, but he couldn't. Then he heard a popping sound. Emma had bitten off his thumb!

Matt in the hospital after losing his thumb to the powerful bite of a moray eel

Emma, the seven-foot-long (2.1-m) moray eel that bit Matt Butcher

DANGER

The area where Matt and his friend were scuba diving is popular with many people because there are lots of beautiful **coral reefs** to see.

Swimmers Beware

Moray eels usually don't attack people. Most of the time they're shy around humans. Then why did Emma bite Matt? The eel was going for the bag of meat, but she accidentally got Matt's hand instead. Moray eels will, however, attack swimmers if they mistake them for food or if they feel threatened. They will also bite divers who poke around in their homes or hiding places.

Matt was lucky, however. He got out of the water alive. After receiving first aid from nearby Navy workers, he was taken to a hospital. The injury would always remind Matt of one important fact: Moray eels have dangerously sharp teeth!

Divers must be careful when they are near moray eels.

A moray's teeth are so sharp that they can easily tear skin.

DANGER

Luckily, Matt's hand didn't become **infected**. After several months, his wound healed. Then Matt underwent an operation, where a doctor removed one of his toes and attached it to his hand—giving Matt a brand-new thumb!

That's a Moray!

It's a good idea to stay away from moray eels because of their super-sharp teeth. However, they're fascinating creatures to watch. Unlike most other fish, they move like snakes in the water. Their bodies wiggle and wave. Why do they swim this way? Moray eels don't have **pectoral fins** like other eels. This makes it hard for them to stay balanced. Often they tilt sideways or swim upside down.

Moray eels come in all sizes. The biggest is the giant moray. It can grow to a length of about 13 feet (4 m). The pygmy moray is the smallest. It's only about 8 inches (20 cm) long. Most adult morays, however, are about 5 feet (1.5 m) in length.

Though moray eels don't have pectoral fins, they do have dorsal and ventral fins along their backs and bottoms. These fins help them move through the water.

dorsal fin

moray eel

ventral fin
(hidden)

conger eel

dorsal fin

ventral fin
(hidden)

pectoral
fin

Many eels, like the conger eel, have dorsal fins, ventral fins, and pectoral fins.

8

The green moray, one of the largest moray eels, is actually blue. The yellow slime on its body makes it look green.

There are more than 200 kinds of moray eels. They come in many different colors and patterns. Though these fish are very dangerous, their bright colors can make them look very beautiful.

Teeth and More Teeth

All morays, whether large or small, have extremely dangerous teeth in their mouths. Most kinds have a few rows of curved teeth with tips that are as sharp as needles. The fish's throat, however, is as deadly as its mouth. Why? Morays have more sharp teeth hidden there!

Scientists made this discovery recently, in 2007. At the University of California, researcher Rita Mehta filmed a moray eating, using high-speed video. When she played it back in slow motion, she saw something come up quickly from the fish's throat. It was a second set of jaws with sharp teeth. Morays use them to pull **prey** down their throats after biting them.

Rita Mehta studying a moray eel

First set
of jaws

Pharyngeal jaws
(second set of jaws)

Pharyngeal
jaws

DANGER

A moray eel captures prey
with its teeth from its first set
of jaws. Then its second set
of jaws, called the pharyngeal
(fa-ren-JEE-uhl) jaws, reaches
up and grabs the prey and
pulls it back into its throat,
swallowing it.

Hunting for Food

Moray eels use their sharp teeth to attack sea animals. Their favorite sea foods are fish, octopus, lobster, and shrimp.

Many morays hunt at night. Scientists are currently researching how they find food. Some think that the eels don't see or hear well so they use their sharp sense of smell to help them find food. When hunting, a moray often sneaks up on a victim that is resting. Other times it hides behind rocks in a coral reef. When prey comes by, the moray darts out and bites down hard!

A moray eel
eating a fish

DANGER

A moray eel's teeth curve back toward its throat. This allows its teeth to grip prey extra tight, making escape nearly impossible.

Moray eels have very few enemies, though sharks sometimes kill them for food.

Angry Looks

Morays can look angry when they open their mouths and show their teeth. Sometimes this means the eels are about to attack. More often, however, they're just breathing.

Like other fish, morays breathe with their **gills**, which take in **oxygen** from water. However, their gills are smaller than other fish. They can't take in as much water. As a result, morays are constantly opening and closing their mouths. This allows them to pump in more water to pass over their gills and give them the oxygen they need to breathe. Sometimes it looks like they're biting the water.

gill opening

After a moray takes in the water it needs to breathe, it closes its mouth. The water passes out of the moray's body through two tiny gill openings on each side of its head.

This moray eel is either ready to attack or simply breathing.

Ocean Homes

Moray eels live in oceans around the world. They stay in warm waters near the **equator**. Some morays swim as deep as 150 feet (46 m). Most, however, stay in **shallow** water.

A moray's home is called its **lair**. Most moray eels live alone and don't share their homes. Many of them make their lairs in the rocky cracks and holes of coral reefs. Thick slime on their skin keeps them from getting cut and scraped as they move around.

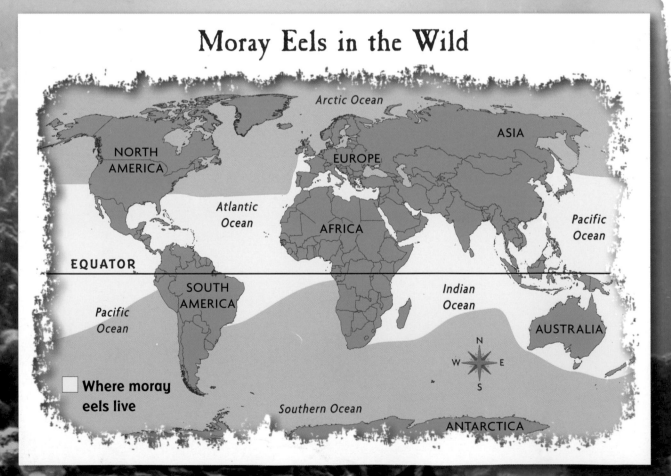

Moray Eels in the Wild

☐ **Where moray eels live**

DANGER

Many morays blend in with the color of the coral reefs around them, making it hard for enemies and prey to spot them.

Baby Morays

During the summer, moray eels **mate** in the warm water. The female lays millions of tiny eggs. Each one is as small as the head of a pin. The eggs float near the top of the water for about ten weeks. The parents don't stay around to protect them, so many eggs are eaten by other animals. The babies that survive and hatch from the eggs are called **larvae**.

Young moray eels, like their parents, make their homes in coral reefs. Soon they, too, will be scaring swimmers and sea animals with their dangerous teeth!

Moray eels
before mating

DANGER

Most morays in
the ocean live 10
to 20 years.

In Case of a Bite

Luckily, most swimmers will never meet up with a moray eel. Every once in a while, though, a person will be attacked. Experts offer this advice to victims of moray eel bites.

1. Do not jerk your hand or other body parts back while the moray's teeth are still dug into your skin. It can make the bite worse.

2. Once you are out of the water, see a doctor immediately.

3. If you cannot get to a doctor right away, wash the wound with soap. Keep it wrapped in a cloth or a bandage so it stays clean and doesn't become infected.

4. After receiving medical treatment, return to the doctor if the wound swells up, stays red and painful, or bleeds.

If a swimmer meets up with a moray eel, the best thing to do is simply ignore it or watch from a distance.

This is how an arm, bitten by a moray eel, looked after the wound was cleaned.

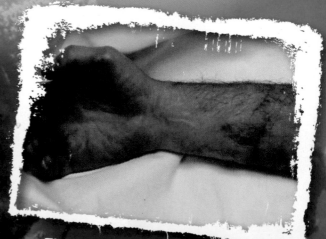

This is how the same arm looked one year after the attack.

DANGER

Moray eels can harm people
in other ways besides biting
them. They have poison in
their flesh like some other
fish, such as barracuda.
People who eat the meat can
become very ill. They may
suffer stomach pains and feel
very weak for several days.

Other Things That Bite

The moray eel is one ocean creature that has a powerful bite. Other kinds of sea animals also have painful and dangerous bites.

Piranhas

- These small, thin fish of South America are famous for being cruel killers.
- Piranhas often travel in groups. They will attack any animal or person that enters their territory.
- Their teeth are shaped like triangles and are razor-sharp along the edges. Piranhas use them to chop their victims into tiny pieces.
- In 1913, while on a hunting trip in Brazil, President Theodore Roosevelt (1901–1909) saw a group of piranhas attack and strip off all the meat on a cow in just a few minutes. Nothing but the animal's skeleton was left.

Barracuda

- These long, slim fish swim in warm ocean waters around the world.
- A barracuda has a big mouth with two sets of razor-sharp teeth. Some teeth are small and shaped like triangles. Other teeth are long and shaped like knives.
- When a barracuda bites, its mouth closes completely, so victims have no chance of escaping.
- Barracuda either swallow their prey whole or use their sharp teeth to cut them into pieces.

Glossary

coral reefs (KOR-uhl REEFS) groups of rock-like structures formed from the skeletons of small sea animals called coral polyps; usually found in shallow tropical waters

equator (i-KWAY-tur) an imaginary line around the middle of Earth, where it is warm all year round

gills (GILZ) the parts of a fish that allow it to breathe underwater

infected (in-FEK-tid) injured and filled with germs

lair (LAIR) a place where some wild animals, such as eels, rest and sleep

larvae (LAR-vee) the young form of animals, such as eels, when they are just born or hatched from eggs

mate (MATE) to come together to have young

oxygen (OK-suh-juhn) an invisible gas found in water or air

pectoral fins (PEK-tuh-ruhl FINZ) flap-like parts located on the sides of a fish that help it to move through the water

prey (PRAY) an animal that is hunted by another animal for food

scuba diving (SKOO-buh DYE-ving) swimming underwater for long periods of time wearing an air tank; the air tank helps a swimmer breathe and connects to the swimmer's mouth by a hose

shallow (SHAL-oh) not very deep

Index

Bibliography

Rake, Jody Sullivan. *Eels*. Mankato, MN: Capstone (2007).

Stone, Lynn M. *Eels*. Vero Beach, FL: Rourke (2005).

Wallace, Karen. *Think of an Eel*. Cambridge, MA: Candlewick Press (2008).

Read More

Gross, Miriam J. *The Moray Eel*. New York: PowerKids Press (2005).

Hirschmann, Kris. *Moray Eels (Creatures of the Sea)*. Detroit, MI: KidHaven Press (2003).

Rothaus, Don P. *Moray Eels*. Chanhassen, MN: The Child's World (2007).

Learn More Online

To learn more about moray eels, visit
www.bearportpublishing.com/AfraidoftheWater

About the Author

Meish Goldish has written more than 200 books for children.
He lives in Brooklyn, New York.